Ohlaf The Krin

Written by
Tod Steward

Illustrated by
Karen Johnson

Thank you Tod and Karen for making our dreams a little sweeter!
Eric & Lisa

ISBN 978-0-692-01124-9
Made in the USA.

Ohlaf H. Olesen was born above his family's bakery in Copenhagen, Denmark. The bakery stood on the sunny side of Bredsgade Street, near the magical Tivoli Gardens. The family lived upstairs.

Ohlaf's whole family worked as bakers. They always had. Ohlaf's first toy was a wooden spoon he used to mix mud pies in the back yard. His mother and father and even his grandfather and grandmother all agreed Ohlaf would make a good baker when he grew up.

In their bakery, Ohlaf's family made coffee cakes, full of creamy custard and piled with apples and cinnamon. They made bread pudding. Of course they baked cakes and special Danish butter cookies. But their specialty was...

Kringle! Ohlaf's family baked kringle filled with chopped apples, or raspberries, or even sweet almond paste. But at that time, kringle did not look as it does today. It was twisted around on itself like a pretzel. In fact, each Danish bakery had a sign of a pretzel shaped kringle outside the door. It made them easier to find.

When he was old enough, Ohlaf's grandmother stood him on a wooden crate at the high workbench where she made candies from thick, sweet almond paste. She showed him how to shape the paste into apples, and lemons, and oranges. She also showed him how to lick the paste from his fingers when they were done. Ohlaf loved to help his grandmother.

As he grew, Ohlaf spent many hours in the bakery. He asked questions. He helped when he could. And when he was eight years old Ohlaf baked his first batch of Danish sugar cookies, all by himself. They were wonderful! Ohlaf's parents were pleased and proud.

When he was not helping in the bakery, Ohlaf went with his mother and father on outings. They walked down the clean, wide streets to the busy harbor. There they waved at the Little Mermaid where she sat on her rock and watched boats of all kinds coming and going.

Sometimes Ohlaf and his parents even visited the wonderful Tivoli Gardens. There they saw clowns and plays and listened to happy music. Ohlaf clapped and laughed all day. When the sun went down, little white lights twinkled on everywhere they looked! Ohlaf was thrilled.

Ohlaf still spent plenty of time in the bakery. He learned all about baking. His mother taught him to mix his bread dough with care. His father taught him how to bake it just right. Grandmother taught him to make fruit filling for tasty treats. Grandfather taught Ohlaf to take his time. Ohlaf enjoyed every minute.

The more time he spent in the bakery, the less time Ohlaf had to play with his friends. In fact, it was sometimes hard to work when he could hear the other children playing outside. But Ohlaf loved to bake with his family. And he loved to make the tasty-sweet bakery treats so many people enjoyed.

And then, one day, Ohlaf's father gave him an official baker's hat. And his very own baker's apron. Ohlaf was so happy he thought he might pop like a balloon. His father said, "Ohlaf, you may only be eight years old. But you are a real baker now." And so he was.

From that day, Ohlaf baked every day except Saturday and Sunday. It was hard work, but he loved it! Everything he learned was a mystery solved. Sometimes he made mistakes. Like when he burned a whole oven full of bread. Of course, Ohlaf's father was angry. But then he helped Ohlaf to make a new batch of bread that turned out well.

When they were done, his father said with a smile, "Very good, Ohlaf. A baker never gives up."

Another time, Ohlaf was making cake batter in the big, metal mixing machine. And he forgot to slow the machine before adding the flour. In only a moment, white flour filled the air like snow. It covered the floor and workbench. It covered Ohlaf, who now looked like a snowman. Ohlaf could only smile and laugh and mix the batter again.

The days went quickly by, full of hard, fun work. Ohlaf learned quickly. He never forgot. What's more, he seemed to have a special touch. One night after the bakery closed, his mother had a talk with his father. His father spoke with Grandmother who talked with Grandfather. They decided Ohlaf would create his very own special treat to sell in the bakery.

Ohlaf began with a simple sugar cookie recipe. But after cutting his dough into circles he put a big spoonful of raspberry filling on top of each one. Then he slid the cookies into the oven. He sat on his stool and waited nervously to see how they would turn out.

The cookies were delicious! As word spread, the bakery filled with customers who bought every one. And then bought them again when Ohlaf made another batch! Grandfather nodded to Grandmother, who whispered to Ohlaf's mother, who leaned over and spoke in her husband's ear. Ohlaf was sitting on a stool at the workbench planning what he would bake the next morning. He wondered what they were whispering about.

“Son, we’re very proud of you,” his father finally said.
“You’ve worked hard,” Grandfather added.
“You’ve become quite a baker!” his mother explained.
“So you will make kringle for the King’s Baking Contest at Tivoli Gardens,” Grandmother said.

Ohlaf was so surprised he fell off his stool. But he climbed back up.
“You’ll have to make it yourself,” she added.
Ohlaf nodded but he was worried. Sugar cookies were one thing. But baking kringle was another. And baking kringle for the big contest at Tivoli Gardens was something else entirely!

Every year the King and Queen of Denmark held a special festival at Tivoli Gardens. It took a whole week to celebrate what made Danish people happy. The King judged music. The Queen judged dancing. And on the morning of the last day, their daughter the Princess Margarethe judged kringle. She awarded a blue ribbon and a solid gold medal to the very best kringle baker. It was the most important contest of the festival.

Three days before the contest, Ohlaf started to make his kringle. First, he mixed enough dough to make two kringle and rolled it out flat. Then he added a layer of butter and folded it over and over before sliding it into the refrigerator to chill. Ohlaf wondered if it really needed to chill for a whole day. "Patience, Ohlaf," Grandfather said.

Early the next day, Ohlaf mixed the fresh raspberry filling for his kringle. Then he pulled the kringle dough out of the refrigerator.

He slowly rolled it flat
again, added another
layer of butter,
and folded it over
and over again.
"Carefully, Ohlaf,"
his father said.
Then they put the
dough back into the
refrigerator. It still
did not look much
like kringle.

Ohlaf still did his daily work. They had a bakery to run! But all the time he thought of his kringle. It had to be wonderful! And there was only one more step before his special kringle was done. Ohlaf had to wake very early in the morning to roll, fill, shape, bake, and frost his kringle with icing so it was perfectly fresh for the contest.

That night Ohlaf dreamt of his kringle. Of the lovely smell. Of the delicious sweetness. He smiled as he slept. Even in his sleep, he could hardly wait for the contest. He had done everything right so far. But, then, he overslept!

He woke in a panic and raced downstairs and pulled the dough from the refrigerator. He tried to roll it out and add the filling and twist the kringle into a pretzel shape. But he was in such a rush he ruined it. He frowned and felt like he might cry. He only had enough dough for one more kringle and he was running out of time. He began to get dizzy.

Ohlaf took a deep breath. His father had told him a baker never gives up. But what could he do? Patience, Ohlaf. Carefully, Ohlaf. He shook his head. Then he looked over at the big bowl of fresh raspberry filling and had an idea.

Ohlaf loved raspberry filling. So he decided to put extra filling in his last kringle.

To do this he carefully shaped his kringle into an "O" instead of a pretzel. When he was done, he slid it into the oven.

Then, he sat down on his stool and wondered if he had done the right thing. After all, no one had ever made a kringle that way before. He closed his eyes and hoped it would turn out well.

Half an hour later, while the sun was still waiting to rise, Ohlaf pulled his oval raspberry kringle from the oven, set it on the workbench and frosted it. It was a lovely golden brown. It smelled fruity and buttery and wonderful. But it was a new shape and Ohlaf was still worried. A moment later his mother and father came down and saw the oval raspberry kringle.

Ohlaf wondered what his parents would say. Had he let them down? But when he told them what had happened, they just smiled. "It smells wonderful," his mother said. His father added, "Don't worry, Ohlaf. It is an odd shape but you worked hard and never gave up. I'm sure the Princess will love it!"

By the time Ohlaf reached Tivoli Gardens with his oval raspberry kringle, the magical old place was full of people. Happy voices rang. Ohlaf and his family made their way to where all the bakers had gathered in their hats and aprons. Soon, the Princess arrived to judge the kringle contest.

Princess Margarethe waved to the crowd. She loved kringle and could not wait to start. First she tasted an almond kringle. Then she tried an apple kringle she liked. Then she took only a nibble from a cream-filled kringle that was too sweet.

She tried small bites of a dozen more while Ohlaf waited and tried to smile. Finally, the Princess reached Ohlaf and his oval raspberry kringle.

"What's that?" the Princess asked politely. "Is it kringle? Shaped like this?" Ohlaf could only nod.
"Yes, your Highness. It is stuffed full of raspberry filling!"

"Oh, I simply love raspberries!" the Princess said with a bright twinkle in her eye. Ohlaf offered her a piece and stepped back. He held his breath. What would she think? What would she say?

The Princess took a nibble. And a larger bite. She smiled at Ohlaf. She smiled at the crowd.

Then she turned to Ohlaf and said, “Wonderful! We must save some for the King and Queen. They’ll love it! This is the best kringle ever!” Ohlaf had won the contest!

His oval raspberry kringle was the best in all of Denmark! His father smiled. His mother gave him a big hug. Ohlaf bowed low to the Princess and said, “Thank you.”

That evening, the awards ceremony began as the sun went down and the little white lights twinkled on all over Tivoli Gardens. Ohlaf stood smiling while the Princess pinned a blue ribbon on his apron and hung the heavy gold medal around his neck.

Nearby, the King and Queen stood with Ohlaf's parents and grandparents. They talked about Ohlaf's kringle. They laughed together like old friends. And the Queen asked, "How early does your bakery open tomorrow?"

The next morning as the sun was beginning to rise, Ohlaf's family got ready to open their bakery. They filled their shelves with warm bread, pastries, and tasty coffee cakes. Ohlaf pulled fresh, oval raspberry kringle from the oven with a smile on his face.

He still wore the gold medal around his neck and the blue ribbon on his apron. They were both covered with flour. When everything was ready, his mother called, "Okay, Ohlaf, it is 7:00 a.m. Go ahead and open the door!"

When Ohlaf opened the door, he nearly fell over backwards. Outside a big crowd had gathered and stood eagerly in line. Right up front stood the King and Queen of Denmark. Very first of all was Princess Margarethe. She smiled and asked, "Do you have any of your wonderful kringle today, Ohlaf?"

Ohlaf nodded. “Oh, yes! The very best!” he said.
And he led the Princess inside.

Ohlaf's Danish Sugar Cookies

1 cup Butter
2 cups Flour
1 cup Sugar
½ teaspoon Baking Soda
1 Egg
½ teaspoon Cream of Tartar
1 teaspoon Vanilla

Cream butter, add sugar and egg. Blend in sifted dry ingredients.

Add vanilla. Place walnut size balls of dough on greased cookie pan and flatten with bottom of glass dipped in sugar.

Bake at 350° for 10 to 12 minutes.

We hope you have enjoyed reading our very first book about Ohlaf, The Kringle Baker. We created this book by including some of our own memories of growing up in our four-generation-family-owned bakery. In this book we share our Danish heritage and appreciation for the life lessons taught to us by our parents and grandparents. For added fun this book includes our good-luck-mouse hidden in one of the illustrations because everyone deserves some good luck each day. Have you found the mouse? Our life has been blessed with good luck, family, friends, traditions, and Kringle.

Eric & Lisa

www.ohdanishbakery.com
Racine, WI
800-709-4009